D0538446

by **Andrew Goldsmith**

Consultant: Alison Howard

BEARPORT
PUBLISHING COMPANY, INC.

New York, New York

Picture credits (t=top; b=bottom; c=center; l=left; r=right): Bookmatrix: 6-7 all, 8-9 all, 18-19 all, 22-23 all, 24-25 all. Natural History Museum: 2b, 4-5 all, 10-11 all, 12-13 all, 14-15 all. Luis Rey: 16-17 all. Pulsar: 20-21 all. Simon Mendez: 26-27 all.

Every effort has been made to trace the copyright holders, and we apologize in advance for any unintentional omissions. We would be pleased to insert the appropriate acknowledgments in any subsequent edition of this publication.

Library of Congress Cataloging-in-Publication Data
Goldsmith, Andrew, 1963-
  Prehistoric beasts / by Andrew Goldsmith.
      p. cm. — (Top 10s)
  Includes index.
  ISBN 1-59716-063-6 (library binding) — ISBN 1-59716-100-4 (pbk.)
   1. Vertebrates, Fossil—Juvenile literature. 2. Herbivores, Fossil—Juvenile literature. 3. Carnivora, Fossil—Juvenile literature. 4. Dinosaurs—Juvenile literature. I. Title. II. Series.

QE842.G65 2006
560—dc22

                                        2005010312

For more information, write to Bearport Publishing Company, Inc., 101 Fifth Avenue, Suite 6R, New York, New York 10003. Printed in the United States of America.

                        2 3 4 5 6 7 8 9 10

CONTENTS

INTRODUCTION

The dinosaurs died out about **65** million years ago. After they were gone, some very large and fierce birds and **mammals** began to appear on Earth. This book presents our Top 10 prehistoric beasts. They were rated on a scale of one to ten in the following categories:

BODY MASS

In this category, we gave the most points to the heaviest animals. In some cases, we were unable to determine weight. For those animals, we used height and length to come up with a score.

SKULL SIZE

The larger the skull, the more points the animal was given. A big skull usually means large jaws or a large **beak**. Either of these features helps an animal get food more easily. A larger skull also provides room for larger eyes. Animals with good eyesight are often good hunters. Sometimes, a large skull means the animal has a large brain. Smarter animals are better hunters.

NO. 9 | MACRAUCHENIA

Macrauchenia (mak-raw-KEE-nee-ah) was a strange-looking beast. It looked like a camel but had a unique, muscular nose. This four-legged creature lived between 7 million and 20,000 years ago. Macrauchenia fossils have only been found in South America. The first Macrauchenia skeleton was discovered in the early 1800s by Englishman Charles Darwin.

BODY MASS
The Macrauchenia was large. It had a long neck, big feet, and 10-foot-long (3 m) legs. It had a trunk like an elephant, only shorter.

SKULL SIZE
The Macrauchenia's head was small. Its nostrils were located at the end of its trunk.

Macrauchenia had legs suited for running fast.

FIGHTING SKILLS

Animals need fighting skills to survive. Points were given for teeth, **tusks**, claws, and kicking power. **Predators** scored high in this category. We also found some plant-eaters, however, that could defend themselves quite well.

SPEED

Predators and **prey** benefit from being able to move quickly. Speed alone, however, is not enough. A speedy animal needs to be able to change direction quickly and easily. It also needs to be able to come to a sudden stop. Our prehistoric animals were given points for speed, **acceleration**, and overall **agility**.

Macrauchenia had a small head.

FIGHTING SKILLS

Macrauchenias were not known for their fighting skills. They easily became the prey of big cats. Their best defense was to run away from trouble.

SPEED

The Macrauchenias' hoof-like feet, each with three toes, helped these animals to run quickly. The design of their ankles and shins allowed them to twist and turn while running.

EXISTED FOR

Macrauchenias existed for about 7 million years.

EXTREME SCORES

Macrauchenias were big but not **aggressive**. Their great strength—running—was used to escape from predators.

BODY MASS 8/10

SKULL SIZE 4/10

FIGHTING SKILLS 2/10

SPEED 8/10

EXISTED FOR 5/10

= TOTAL SCORE 27/50

EXISTED FOR

All animals in this book are extinct—none of their kind is still alive. We gave extra points for animals that lived the longest ago. We gave animals with long life spans more points than other animals. The longer a **species** survived on Earth, the more points it got. Extra points were given to animals that lived during times with harsh conditions, such as the **Ice Age**.

9

Gastornis (gas-TOR-niss) was a giant, meat-eating bird that lived in thick forests. The many trees allowed the bird to **ambush** its prey. Gastornis, one of the largest animals of its time, lived 56–41 million years ago. A Frenchman named Gaston Planté first discovered Gastornis. He found its **fossils** in Paris, France.

SKULL SIZE

Gastornis had an enormous beak. Most scientists say the beak was used for cracking nuts. Others suggest that it may have been used to crush bones.

The powerful beak of Gastornis was used to kill its prey.

FIGHTING SKILLS

Gastornis probably used its huge beak to grab animals and then crush their **spines**. This action **paralyzed** the prey, which kept them from struggling. Gastornis had a huge appetite.

SPEED

Gastornis was a very slow animal.
It probably couldn't catch fast-running prey.
So, it had to take its **victims** by surprise.

BODY MASS

Gastornis was about 6 feet (2 m) tall.
It had very small wings but could not fly.

EXISTED FOR

This species of bird
lived on Earth for
approximately
9 million years.

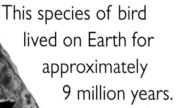

**Gastornis was
probably a
relative of
the dinosaurs.**

Gastornis was a giant of a bird. It was a beast that was known for its surprise attacks and strong beak.

BODY MASS
3/10

SKULL SIZE
5/10

FIGHTING SKILLS
6/10

SPEED
6/10

EXISTED FOR
6/10

= TOTAL SCORE
26/50

Macrauchenia (mak-raw-KEE-nee-ah) was a strange-looking beast. It looked like a camel but had a unique, muscular nose. This four-legged creature lived between 7 million and 20,000 years ago. Macrauchenia fossils have only been found in South America. The first Macrauchenia skeleton was discovered in the early 1800s by Englishman Charles Darwin.

BODY MASS

The Macrauchenia was large. It had a long neck, big feet, and 10-foot-long (3 m) legs. It had a trunk like an elephant, only shorter.

SKULL SIZE

The Macrauchenia's head was small. Its nostrils were located at the end of its trunk.

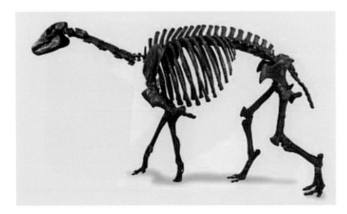

Macrauchenia had legs suited for running fast.

Macrauchenia had a small head.

FIGHTING SKILLS

Macrauchenias were not known for their fighting skills. They easily became the prey of big cats. Their best defense was to run away from trouble.

SPEED

The Macrauchenias' hoof-like feet, each with three toes, helped these animals to run quickly. The design of their ankles and shins allowed them to twist and turn while running.

EXISTED FOR

Macrauchenias existed for about 7 million years.

Macrauchenias were big but not **aggressive**. Their great strength—running—was used to escape from predators.

BODY MASS 8/10
SKULL SIZE 4/10
FIGHTING SKILLS 2/10
SPEED 8/10
EXISTED FOR 5/10

= TOTAL SCORE 27/50

These tigers were the fiercest of all Ice Age **carnivores**. They lived between 1.6 million and 11,000 years ago. They probably looked like today's lions, although they were heavier and a little shorter. These tigers also hunted in groups. Fossils of saber-toothed tigers have been found in Africa and both North and South America.

BODY MASS

The saber-toothed tiger weighed about 440 pounds (200 kg). It was almost 4 feet (1 m) tall at the shoulder.

These tigers were named for their large front teeth. Saber is the name of a kind of curved sword.

SKULL SIZE

The saber-toothed tiger's skull was about 12 inches (30 cm) long. It had two huge **canine** teeth, each about 7 inches (18 cm) long. The tiger could open its mouth more widely than today's tigers. This gave the animal a fierce look.

SPEED

This beast was not a fast runner. It had powerful but short front legs. Its body was made for pouncing on prey.

Saber-toothed tigers had long, powerful teeth.

FIGHTING SKILLS

The saber-toothed tiger probably attacked large animals from a hiding place. The animal also probably wounded its prey with the long, sharp canine teeth. Then, as the victim bled to death, the tiger would eat it.

EXISTED FOR

Saber-toothed tigers lived on Earth for about 1.8 million years.

Extra long teeth and a powerful body made this animal a fearsome killer.

BODY MASS
2/10

SKULL SIZE
6/10

FIGHTING SKILLS
8/10

SPEED
7/10

EXISTED FOR
5/10

= TOTAL SCORE
28/50

Andrewsarchus (and-rooz-ARK-uss) looked like a wolf. It had four short legs and a long body, tail, and nose. Scientists believe that Andrewsarchus was the largest meat-eating land mammal that ever lived. Its fossils were first discovered in Mongolia in 1923 by Kan Chuen Pao.

BODY MASS

The body of Andrewsarchus was very long—up to 16 feet (5 m). It stood about 6 feet (2 m) tall at the shoulder. It probably weighed close to a ton (1 metric ton).

SKULL SIZE

This animal's huge skull was almost 3 feet (1 m) across. Its sharp teeth could easily crush bones.

FIGHTING SKILLS

Andrewsarchus probably hunted along riverbanks. It may have preyed on turtles and other water animals. It may also have been a **scavenger**.

Powerful jaws and strong teeth could easily crush turtle shells.

SPEED

The animal had a stiff backbone and short legs. It was not a fast or agile runner.

Andrewsarchus was a relative of hoofed animals. It was also a distant relative of whales.

EXISTED FOR

Andrewsarchuses existed on Earth for about 16 million years.

Goldilocks would have been really afraid if she'd seen the size of Andrewsarchus's teeth. Luckily, she'd probably be able to outrun this animal.

BODY MASS
4/10

SKULL SIZE
7/10

FIGHTING SKILLS
8/10

SPEED
3/10

EXISTED FOR
7/10

= TOTAL SCORE
29/50

Chalicotheres (KAL-ik-oh-theerz) were related to rhinoceroses and horses. Remains of two types of the animal have been found. One, a goat-like beast, lived on the plains. The other, more like a gorilla, lived in forests and walked on its knuckles. Fossils have been found in North America, Europe, and Asia.

BODY MASS

This animal was fairly tall. Males were probably about 9 feet (3 m) when standing upright.

SKULL SIZE

The Chalicothere had an extremely large skull for its body size. It used its back teeth to grind up soft plants. It did not have front teeth.

FIGHTING SKILLS

The animal's long claws were not used to attack prey. They were probably used to dig in the soil and to pull down leaves and vines. This plant-eater may have extended its long arms to defend itself against attacks.

Like modern gorillas, some Chalicotheres probably used their long arms to pull leaves from trees.

A jawbone of a Chalicothere, discovered in a riverbed in Nebraska

SPEED

With such long claws, Chalicotheres were probably not fast runners.

EXISTED FOR

Chalicotheres existed for about 34 to 50 million years.

Though the claws on these animals looked scary, Chalicotheres were probably only a threat to plants.

BODY MASS
5/10

SKULL SIZE
7/10

FIGHTING SKILLS
4/10

SPEED
4/10

EXISTED FOR
10/10

= TOTAL SCORE
30/50

Ambulocetus (am-byu-lo-**SEE**-tus) had the ability to walk on land and swim in water. This beast was so strong that it could easily kill larger animals. Though it was an early kind of whale, it looked more like an angry crocodile. It lived about **49 million years ago**, in what is now **Pakistan, India, and Egypt**. Its remains were first discovered and named by **Hans Thewissen**.

The name Ambulocetus means "walking whale."

BODY MASS

Ambulocetus weighed around 650 pounds (295 kg). It was about 10 feet (3 m) long.

SKULL SIZE

Ambulocetus had a whale-like skull except for the nose. It had powerful jaws and whale-like teeth.

FIGHTING SKILLS

Ambulocetus probably ambushed its prey. Then, it grabbed the animal in its teeth and held it underwater until it drowned.

Scientists know Ambulocetus was a kind of whale because of the shape of its teeth and ears.

SPEED

Ambulocetus was an **amphibian**. It was a good swimmer, but not very fast on land.

EXISTED FOR

This animal survived about 3.5 million years on Earth.

Like today's crocodiles, this animal was probably a super killer.

BODY MASS
6/10

SKULL SIZE
7/10

FIGHTING SKILLS
6/10

SPEED
9/10

EXISTED FOR
5/10

= TOTAL SCORE
33/50

Indricotheres (IN-drik-oh-theerz) are the largest land mammals that ever lived. Though related to today's rhinoceroses, Indricotheres ate from treetops like giraffes. Fossil remains of the animals have been found in Europe and Asia.

BODY MASS

These beasts were gigantic. They could weigh over 17 tons (15 metric tons). They could grow to almost 15 feet (5 m) tall.

SKULL SIZE

The Indricothere's large head had a small brain. It had a long neck, but its skull was lightweight. The animal had flat grinding teeth in the back of its mouth.

FIGHTING SKILLS

Indricotheres probably fought like giraffes. First, they would have entwined their necks. Then they would have swung their heads against each other.

Indricotheres, like today's rhinos, probably had thick leathery skin.

SPEED

They may have been able to run but were not known for their speed.

EXISTED FOR

This species survived for about 14 million years on Earth.

Indricotheres were a little bigger than the largest elephants alive today.

It's lucky for other animals that these huge beasts ate plants for food.

BODY MASS
10/10

SKULL SIZE
8/10

FIGHTING SKILLS
6/10

SPEED
3/10

EXISTED FOR
7/10

= TOTAL SCORE
34/50

Mammoths (MAM-oths) were very similar to today's elephants. There were several species of mammoths that ranged in height from about 6–12 feet (2–4 m). These beasts probably lived in groups that included only females and the young. Fossil remains of mammoths have been found in Europe, Asia, and North America. Mammoths became extinct about 11,000 years ago.

BODY MASS

The Columbian mammoth was the largest of these animals. It grew to about 12 feet (4 m) tall at the shoulder. It weighed as much as 10 tons (9 metric tons).

SKULL SIZE

A mammoth head was very large and dome shaped. Great tusks, as long as 10–16 feet (3–5 m), grew from the skull. Most mammoths seem to have had a hump behind their heads.

FIGHTING SKILL

Tusks were the main weapons that these plant-eaters used to defend themselves. The tusks were also probably used to dig for food.

When mammoths lost all of their teeth (left), they died of starvation.

These Ice Age giants with huge tusks racked up some impressive scores.

BODY MASS
9/10

SKULL SIZE
10/10

FIGHTING SKILLS
6/10

SPEED
5/10

EXISTED FOR
5/10

= TOTAL SCORE
35/50

SPEED

Like elephants, mammoths would not have been able to run, jump, or gallop. They were easy prey for saber-toothed tigers.

EXISTED FOR

Mammoths survived for about 1.7 million years on Earth.

Several well-preserved woolly mammoth bodies have been found in Siberia. They had been frozen for thousands of years.

Phorusrhacos (FOR-uss-RAH-kuss) was a bird that could catch and eat an animal the size of a camel. It was one of the largest birds that ever existed on Earth. It belongs to a group called the "terror birds." These creatures had claws on the ends of their wings. Fossils of Phorusrhacos have been found in Argentina and North America.

BODY MASS

These beasts weighed around 287 pounds (130 kg). They were over 8 feet (2 m) tall.

SKULL SIZE

The head of Phorusrhacos was as large as a horse's head. Its skull was over 2 feet (61 cm) long.

SPEED

Phorusrhacos was a fast runner because of its long legs.

Phorusrhacos, like other "terror birds," did not fly.

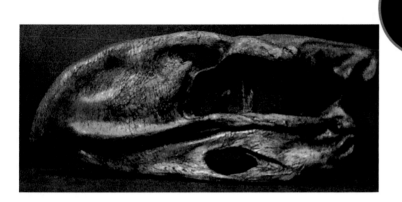

The Phorusrhacos used its fearsome beak to smash prey.

A fast runner with a deadly beak, not many prey escaped this bird's attacks alive.

EXISTED FOR

Phorusrhacos survived on Earth for about 27 million years.

FIGHTING SKILLS

These birds were so fast that they could catch most prey they went after. They had huge, sharp beaks to tear and cut their prey. These deadly animals were the top predator of their time.

BODY MASS 5/10

SKULL SIZE 7/10

FIGHTING SKILLS 6/10

SPEED 10/10

EXISTED FOR 9/10

= TOTAL SCORE 37/50

Entelodonts (en-TELL-oh-dahnts) are related to today's pigs. They were so dangerous that they sometimes grabbed other Entelodonts's heads in their mouths. They probably ate almost any plant or animal they found. They chewed plant roots with their strong back teeth to get water in the dry season.

BODY MASS

Entelodonts were similar in size to buffalo. The largest of these beasts were almost 7 feet (2 m) tall at the shoulder.

SKULL SIZE

Their skulls were over 3 feet (1 m) long. The animals could crush bones with their jaws. Their mouths had many huge teeth and their skulls were covered with strange bony knobs.

FIGHTING SKILLS

Entelodont skulls have been found with gashes from other Entelodonts's teeth. Sometimes these gashes were between the eyes and close to 1 inch (3 cm) deep. Clearly, these beasts were fierce fighters.

The size of an Entelodont's teeth and jaws show how damaging the animal's attacks could be.

EXISTED FOR

Entelodonts survived for approximately 20 million years on Earth.

Entelodonts probably had little hair, like today's large pigs.

SPEED

Entelodonts belonged to the same group as Dinohyus, another similar animal that was a fast runner. Entelodonts's long legs mean that they could also probably run fast.

EXTREME SCORES

We have a winner! This perfect beast had a huge skull and great fighting skills. It could even bite off the entire head of another Entelodont.

BODY MASS
7 / 10

SKULL SIZE
9 / 10

FIGHTING SKILLS
10 / 10

SPEED
7 / 10

EXISTED FOR
8 / 10

= TOTAL SCORE
41 / 50

Choosing just ten prehistoric beasts for this book was very difficult. Here are five beasts that didn't quite make the final list.

DESMOSTYLIANS

The Desmostylians were a very strange group of mammals. They lived about 35 million years ago. They were about the same size as today's horses. They lived in shallow water along coastlines. They may have walked along the seabed, while using their strange teeth to dig out shellfish. The Desmostylians were not closely related to any of the mammals that exist today.

MEGATHERIUM

Megatherium was a gigantic sloth that only became extinct about 10,000 years ago. This mammal lived in South America. It grew to more than 20 feet (6 m) in length. Megatherium was an **herbivore** that fed mainly on the leaves and shoots of trees. It walked on all fours. However, it could stand up on its back legs to reach the higher branches.

ARSINOITHERIUM

Arsinoitherium was a horned mammal. It lived in Africa about 35 million years ago. Despite its appearance, it was not related to today's rhinoceros. The twin horns of Arsinoitherium were made of bone and were a part of the animal's skull. The horn of a rhinoceros, however, is not part of the skull. The horn is made from tightly compressed hair.

STEGODON

Stegodon lived in Africa and Asia about 10–12 million years ago. It was related to mammoths. It had the same long trunk as today's elephants. Its tusks, however, tended to be longer and much straighter. The longest fossil Stegodon tusks that have so far been discovered were each more than 10 feet (3 m) in length.

BULLOCKORNIS

Bullockornis was a giant duck that lived in Australia about 20 million years ago. It had long, powerful legs. It stood about 10 feet (3 m) tall. Although Bullockornis was a kind of duck, it did not have a flat duck's bill. Instead, it had a large, curved beak. The beak was most likely used to tear strips of flesh from dead animals.

NO. 10 GASTORNIS

Extreme Scores

Body Mass	3
Skull Size	5
Fighting Skills	6
Speed	6
Existed For	6

TOTAL SCORE
26/50

NO. 9 MACRAUCHENIA

Extreme Scores

Body Mass	8
Skull Size	4
Fighting Skills	2
Speed	8
Existed For	5

TOTAL SCORE
27/50

NO. 8 SABER-TOOTHED TIGER

Extreme Scores

Body Mass	2
Skull Size	6
Fighting Skills	8
Speed	7
Existed For	5

TOTAL SCORE
28/50

NO. 7 ANDREWSARCHUS

Extreme Scores

Body Mass	4
Skull Size	7
Fighting Skills	8
Speed	3
Existed For	7

TOTAL SCORE
29/50

NO. 6 CHALICOTHERE

Extreme Scores

Body Mass	5
Skull Size	7
Fighting Skills	4
Speed	4
Existed For	10

TOTAL SCORE
30/50

NO. 5 AMBULOCETUS

Extreme Scores

Body Mass	6
Skull Size	7
Fighting Skills	6
Speed	9
Existed For	5

TOTAL SCORE
33 / 50

NO. 4 INDRICOTHERE

Extreme Scores

Body Mass	10
Skull Size	8
Fighting Skills	6
Speed	3
Existed For	7

TOTAL SCORE
34 / 50

NO. 3 MAMMOTH

Extreme Scores

Body Mass	9
Skull Size	10
Fighting Skills	6
Speed	5
Existed For	5

TOTAL SCORE
35 / 50

NO. 2 PHORUSRHACOS

Extreme Scores

Body Mass	5
Skull Size	7
Fighting Skills	6
Speed	10
Existed For	9

TOTAL SCORE
37 / 50

NO. 1 ENTELODONT

Extreme Scores

Body Mass	7
Skull Size	9
Fighting Skills	10
Speed	7
Existed For	8

TOTAL SCORE
41 / 50

acceleration (ak-*sel*-uh-RAY-shun) the act of getting faster and faster

aggressive (uh-GRESS-iv) acting in a threatening or fierce way

agility (uh-JIL-uh-tee) the ability to move quickly and easily

ambush (AM-bush) to hide and then suddenly attack

amphibian (am-FIB-ee-uhn) an animal that lives part of its life in water and part on land

beak (BEEK) the hard, horn-shaped part of a bird's mouth

canine (KAY-nine) one of the sharp, pointy teeth found on the sides of the upper or lower jaws

carnivores (KAR-nuh-*vorz*) meat-eating animals

fossils (FOSS-uhlz) the remains of plants or animals, such as bones, that have turned to rock, or imprints made by plants or animals, such as footprints, that are preserved in rock

herbivore (HUR-buh-*vor*) plant-eating animal

Ice Age (EYESS AJE) any period of time during which ice sheets covered a large part of Earth's surface; the most recent Ice Age lasted from about 2 million to 11 thousand years ago

mammals (MAM-uhlz) animals that are warm-blooded, nurse their young with milk, and have hair or fur on their skin

paralyzed (PA-ruh-lized) made unable to move

predators (PRED-uh-turz) animals that hunt other animals for food

prey (PRAY) animals that are hunted or caught for food

scavenger (SKAV-uhn-jur) an animal that finds food by searching for dead animals

species (SPEE-sheez) groups that animals or plants are divided into according to similar characteristics

spines (SPINEZ) backbones

tusks (TUHSKS) long, pointed teeth, such as those on an elephant or walrus, that are often used for fighting or digging

victims (VIK-tuhmz) animals or people that are hurt, injured, or killed by other animals or people